Awesome Science Experiments
for Kids

www.futuresmartminds.com

Welcome to **FutureSmartMinds**, *where young minds are ignited with curiosity and a passion for STEM learning! We're thrilled you've chosen "**Future Scientist**" to embark on this exciting journey.*

*Your feedback means the world to us! If "**Future Scientist**" has inspired your young scientist or brought educational joy to your family, please consider sharing your thoughts on Amazon. Your review will help other parents and budding scientists discover the wonders of this book.*

**Scan to Rate
Us on Amazon**

*Your purchase not only opens up a world of science and discovery for your child but also supports our mission to nurture the next generation of innovators and critical thinkers. We believe that learning science should be engaging, hands-on, and fun, which is why "**Future Scientist**" is filled with mind-blowing experiments and captivating knowledge.*

Thank you for joining us on this STEM adventure, and here's to a future filled with endless possibilities!

*Warm regards,
The* **FutureSmartMinds** *Team*

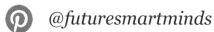
www.futuresmartminds.com

Email: FutureSmartMindsKids@gmail.com

@futuresmartminds

@futuresmartminds

@ futuresmartminds

**Scan to visit
our website**

Contents

(1) Sun-Baked Sweet Treats

Get ready to harness the power of the sun! Have you ever wondered how the sun helps plants grow or warms up our planet? In this experiment, you'll use the sun's energy to cook up a delicious snack. Imagine making your very own dessert with nothing but a few simple materials and the mighty sun as your oven! This experiment is not only about creating a yummy treat but also about understanding how solar energy works. Are you ready to watch the magic happen right before your eyes? Let's get cooking with solar power!

Material

- An empty pizza or cake box
- Aluminum foil
- Black sheet of paper
- Clear plastic wrap
- Glue and tape
- Scissors or a utility knife
- Graham crackers
- Marshmallow
- Chocolate
- Wooden skewers

Instructions

Step 1 Cut a three sided flap on the top of the empty pizza box, cut 2-3" from all sides	**Step 2** Use glue to cover the inside of the flap with aluminum foil	**Step 3** Place a black sheet of paper on the bottom of the pizza box
Step 4 Put your graham crackers, topped with marshmallow and chocolate, onto the black paper inside the box	**Step 5** Tape layers of clear plastic wrap on top of your s'more across the opening you cut in the lid	**Step 6** Close the lid with the flap propped open with the wooden skewers.

Step 7	Step 8	Step 9
Place the solar oven outside in the direct sunlight such that the open flap faces the sun. Try to avoid any shadow	Check on the marshmallow and chocolate every 15 minutes until they are melted. Remove the black paper and your s'mores and wait for them to cool for a few minutes	Place the other graham cracker on top, press them together, and enjoy your energy-efficient s'mores

Illustrations

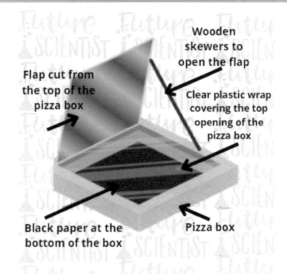

Flap cut from the top of the pizza box

Wooden skewers to open the flap

Clear plastic wrap covering the top opening of the pizza box

Black paper at the bottom of the box

Pizza box

Science

😊 **Solar Energy**: The radiant energy emitted by the sun is the primary source for this experiment. It is what makes the entire process of cooking possible, representing the start of our solar cooking journey.

💧 **Conversion of Solar Energy to Thermal Energy**: Imagine a sunbeam striking the dark surfaces inside the solar oven, similar to how a magnifying glass might focus light to heat a spot. This absorption and conversion of light to heat are crucial for cooking the s'mores.

🏠 **Insulation and Greenhouse Effect**: The plastic wrap acts like the windows of a greenhouse, letting light in and trapping heat. The insulation, akin to a blanket, keeps the heat snug and warm inside our pizza box 'mini-greenhouse.'

(2) Magic Milk

Prepare to be a kitchen magician as you transform a simple dish of milk into a dazzling display of swirling colors! With just a few ingredients like whole milk, dish soap, and food coloring, you can create your very own milk fireworks. Watch as colors dance and mix in ways you've never seen before. This experiment isn't just fun, it's a colorful adventure right in your kitchen. So, get your materials ready and let's turn that milk into a whirling spectacle of color!

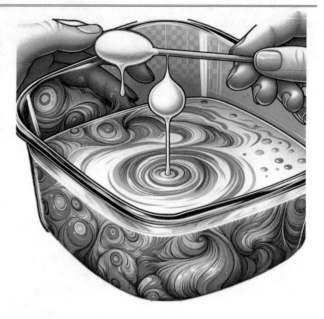

Material

- A variety of milk, such as whole milk, 2% milk, 1% milk, skim milk, and half and half milk
- A flat bottom container with raised sides, such as a baking dish or a paper plate

- Cotton swabs
- Dish soap
- Food colouring
- Small bowl

Instructions

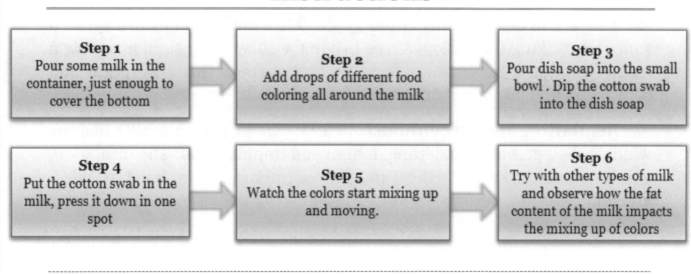

Step 1
Pour some milk in the container, just enough to cover the bottom

Step 2
Add drops of different food coloring all around the milk

Step 3
Pour dish soap into the small bowl . Dip the cotton swab into the dish soap

Step 4
Put the cotton swab in the milk, press it down in one spot

Step 5
Watch the colors start mixing up and moving.

Step 6
Try with other types of milk and observe how the fat content of the milk impacts the mixing up of colors

Science

Milk Composition: Milk is more than just a drink; it's a mixture of minerals, vitamins, proteins, and fats. Each of these ingredients plays a role in our experiment, especially the fats!

Soap's Role: Soap is like a superhero for cleaning, known for its ability to tackle grease and dirt. When it comes to milk, soap has a special mission: to break down fats.

Chasing Fats: When soap meets milk, it's like a chase scene! Soap molecules hunt down fat molecules in the milk. They surround and capture them, forming tiny clusters known as micelles.

Breaking Tension: The soap doesn't just capture fats; it also breaks the milk's surface tension. This is like popping the invisible balloons on the milk's surface, causing all the colorful commotion.

Color Dance: As the soap disrupts the milk's surface tension and chases fats, it stirs the milk, creating a whirlwind of color. The food coloring swirls and mixes, creating our magic of colors.

Fat Content Effect: Not all milk is the same! The more fat in the milk, the more there is for soap to chase. This means in whole milk, you'll see a more dramatic color dance than in skim milk.

Explore further

Soap Quantity Variations: Experiment with varying the amount of soap you dip into the milk. Use less, then more, and observe how the speed and pattern of color mixing change. Does more soap mean faster swirling colors, or is there a point where it doesn't make much difference?

Liquid Laboratory: Replace milk with other liquids like olive oil, water, or coconut milk. What happens when you add food coloring and soap to these liquids? Note the differences or similarities in how the colors move or don't move. What does this tell you about the properties of these liquids compared to milk?

(3) Elephant Toothpaste

Get ready for an exciting chemical adventure with our 'Elephant Toothpaste' experiment! Watch in awe as you create a frothy, colorful foam that looks like a giant toothpaste fit for an elephant's brushing routine. This fun experiment will guide you through a fascinating chemical reaction, teaching you about catalysts and exothermic reactions. Prepare for a bubbly explosion of science that's as educational as it is entertaining. Put on your safety gear, and let's create a spectacular foamy fountain!

Material

- 16 oz plastic soda bottle
- 1/2 cup of 12% solution hydrogen peroxide liquid (labelled as 40-volume)*
- 1 Tablespoon or a sachet of dry yeast (around 1/4 oz)
- 3 Tablespoons of warm water
- 1 Tablespoon of liquid dish soap
- Food colouring
- Small cup
- Safety goggles**
- Safety gloves**

Hydrogen peroxide can irritate skin and eyes.

**Wear your safety goggles and gloves during the experiment and ask an adult to pour hydrogen peroxide solution.*

Instructions

Step 1
Gather your materials and put on your safety goggles and gloves.

Step 2
Add a tablespoon of liquid dish soap into the bottle.

Step 3
Add 8 to 15 drops of food coloring into the bottle (use one color only for best results!).

Step 4
swish the bottle around a bit to mix the ingredients.

Step 5
In a separate small cup, mix your yeast with the warm water for at least 30 seconds. It should be about the consistency of melted ice cream. Add more warm water if needed to get the right consistency.

Step 6
Pour the yeast/hot water mixture into the bottle and take a step back.

Step 7
Watch the elephant toothpaste foam fountain forming!

Science

 Hydrogen Peroxide (H2O2): Commonly used by hairdressers as a bleaching agent, hydrogen peroxide is similar to water (H2O) but has an extra oxygen atom. It's this extra oxygen that makes it so reactive and useful in both beauty and industrial applications.

Decomposition Reaction: Hydrogen peroxide is unstable and breaks down into water (H_2O) and oxygen (O_2) gas. This breakdown is a natural process but happens very slowly. The equation is: $2H_2O_2 \rightarrow 2H_2O + O_2$.

Catalyst - Yeast: Yeast contains an enzyme that accelerates the decomposition of hydrogen peroxide into water and oxygen. This fast release of oxygen creates the frothy foam that resembles toothpaste.

Oxygen Bubbles: The oxygen escapes as tiny bubbles, which get trapped by the dish soap added to the mixture, forming the characteristic foam.

Exothermic Reaction: As the hydrogen peroxide breaks down, it releases energy in the form of heat, making this an exothermic reaction. This is why the foam might feel warm!

Safe Cleanup: The foam is simply water, soap, and oxygen, making it safe and easy to clean up after the fun is over.

Explore further

Yeast Variations: Adjust the amount of yeast you use in the experiment. Experiment with using more or less than the suggested amount. Observe and note how the quantity of yeast affects the volume and speed of the foam production.

Bottle Size: Conduct the experiment using bottles of different sizes. Does a larger bottle create more foam, or does it simply spread out? Compare and contrast the results to understand how container volume impacts the reaction.

Dry Yeast Direct: Try adding dry yeast directly into the hydrogen peroxide solution without mixing it with warm water first. Does this change the reaction's speed or the foam's texture? Record your observations.

Temperature Test: Perform the experiment at different temperatures - perhaps once with cold ingredients and once with ingredients at room temperature. Note any differences in the reaction rate or foam produced due to temperature changes.

"Science is not only a disciple of reason but also one of romance and passion."

- Stephen Hawking
A renowned theoretical physicist who emphasized the importance of emotion and passion in pursuing scientific understanding.

"Somewhere, something incredible is waiting to be known."

- Carl Sagan

An astronomer and author, inspired many to seek the unknown and embrace the vastness of the universe.

"The important thing is to never stop questioning."

- Albert Einstein
One of the most famous physicists, always encouraged curiosity and continuous questioning as a way to learn and discover.

(4) The Floating Egg

Dive into the curious world of density with our 'Floating Egg' experiment! Normally, an egg will sink right to the bottom of a glass of water. But can we make it float instead? By turning your kitchen into a science lab, you'll see the surprising effects of salt on water's density. This simple yet captivating experiment will teach you about the buoyancy of objects and show you how everyday ingredients can reveal extraordinary science. Get ready to explore the floating mysteries of density and buoyancy!

Material

+ One egg
+ An empty glass
+ Tap water
+ 6-10 tablespoon of salt
+ A tablespoon

Instructions

Step 1
Pour tap water into the glass until it is half full

Step 2
Drop an egg in the glass of water and check it sinks or floats

Step 3
Add salt to the water using one tablespoon of salt at a time and stir gently. Keep adding salt until the egg floats

Science

● **Egg Density**: The egg is denser than tap water, meaning more molecules are packed into the same space. This density causes it to sink in pure water as it is heavier per unit of volume.

◗ **Water Density**: Tap water has its own density, determined by how closely packed its molecules are. Initially, this density is less than the egg's; hence, the egg sinks.

▬ **Salt Increases Density**: When you add salt (NaCl) to the water, it dissolves and increases the water's density by adding more molecules into the mix. The more salt you add, the denser the water becomes.

⬆ **Floating Threshold**: Once the water's density exceeds that of the egg, the egg starts to float. This is because the egg is now less dense than the surrounding salty water.

◖ **Layering Effect**: If you carefully pour fresh tap water into the salty water without mixing, it will layer on top. The less-dense fresh water floats above the denser salty water, demonstrating how different fluids can layer based on density.

👀 **Observation and Adjustment**: By adjusting the amount of salt, you can see the egg sink, float, or even suspend in the middle of the glass. This observation shows the direct impact of density on buoyancy.

Explore further

Alternative Liquids: Replace the tap water with other liquids like vinegar, vegetable oil, or sugar water. Follow the same steps you used with water and note how much salt (if at all) is needed to make the egg float in these different fluids. Observe and record the differences in buoyancy and behavior of the egg.

Temperature Test: Conduct the experiment using water at different temperatures. Try one with ice-cold water and another with warm water. Measure and compare the amount of salt needed to make the egg float in each. Discuss how temperature affects the solubility of salt and the density of water.

Fun Facts: Density

Density: is the amount of mass contained in a unit of volume. High-density objects are heavy and compact, whereas low-density objects are light and take up a lot of space.

For example, Box (3) in the figure has more density than Boxes (1) and (2) since it has more particles compacted in the same volume!

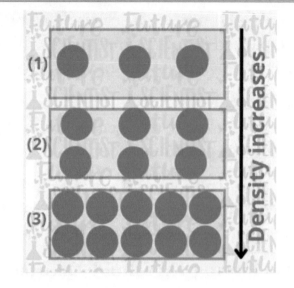

How do we find the density of an object?

To find the density of an object, we need to know its volume and mass.

Formula

$$\text{Density } (\rho) = \frac{\text{Mass (M)}}{\text{Volume (V)}}$$

Units

$$\frac{\text{lbs}}{\text{ft}^3} \text{ or } \frac{\text{kg}}{\text{m}^3}$$

Mass measures how much matter is in an object, measured in lbs or kg. Mass is not the same as weight. **Weight** is a force of gravity applied to an object, measured in Newton (N). A scale on the moon would measure different weights for the same object than a scale on Earth since the strength of gravity is different! However, the mass of the object stays the same.

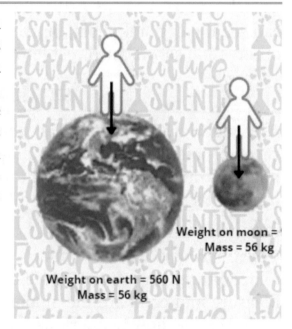

Weight on moon = Mass = 56 kg

Weight on earth = 560 N
Mass = 56 kg

Volume is like the invisible bubble of space that an object fills up, measured in cubic feet (ft³) or cubic meters (m³). Imagine filling a balloon; as you blow air into it, it expands to occupy more space. That space it takes up is its volume. You can calculate the volume of a box-shaped object by multiplying its length, width, and height together. Whether it's a box, a balloon, or even a drop of water, volume tells us how much three-dimensional space any object occupies.

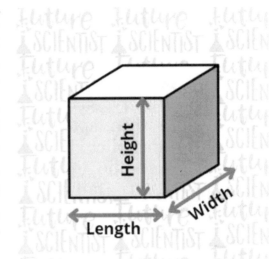

Brick vs. Styrofoam:

A brick is heavy and has high density because its particles are tightly packed with a lot of mass. Conversely, Styrofoam is light with low density due to its loosely packed particles and lesser mass.

Float or Sink:

Density acts like the decision-maker for whether an object will float or sink in water. Objects with a density less than water, like Styrofoam, sponge, and cork, will float. However, objects denser than water, like metal, concrete, and glass, will sink.

Liquid Layers:

Different liquids have different densities. When you mix them, the one with higher density will sit at the bottom. For instance, adding salt to water increases its density, making it denser than plain water.

Temperature & Pressure Impact:

Density isn't static; it changes with temperature and pressure. When heated, most substances expand and become less dense. Similarly, increasing pressure typically makes substances more compact and denser.

(5) Musical Water Glasses

Step into the role of a musical maestro with our 'Musical Water Glasses' experiment! Every glass sings a different note when tapped, and you can control the pitch by changing what's inside the glass. This experiment turns ordinary water glasses into a symphony of sound, allowing you to compose your melodies by simply tapping the glasses with a spoon. Fill each glass with varying amounts of water and add a dash of color for a visual treat. Get ready to discover the music in every pour and learn about the science of sound waves!

Material

- 6 water glasses
- Tap water
- 6 different food colouring
- Wooden or metal spoon

Instructions

Step 1
Fill the 6 glasses with different amount of water. The first one should have a little amount of water and the last one full

Step 2
Tap on the glasses with the spoon and observe the sound

Step 3
Try to create your own tune by tapping on the glasses in a certain order

Step 4
Find a tune that produces simple notes. Color the glasses that produced the notes with different food colors

Step 5
Write down a series of colored dashes on a paper that made up your tune

Step 6
Create more tunes using different combinations of the colored water glasses and write them down

Science

🥄 **Tapping Tones**: When you tap a glass with a spoon, it vibrates, creating sound waves. These vibrations are what produce the musical tones you hear.

💧 **Water Levels**: The amount of water in each glass affects the pitch of the sound. A glass filled with more water will vibrate slower and produce a lower tone, while a glass with less water will vibrate faster and emit a higher tone.

🔊 **Sound Waves**: The vibrations from the glass transfer to the water, creating sound waves that travel through the air to your ears. Changing the water level changes the speed of the vibrations and, thus, the pitch of the sound.

🎵 **Pitch Variation**: The pitch, or how high or low the sound is, changes with the amount of water in the glass. More water means a deeper pitch, while less water results in a higher pitch. This is due to the length of the waves produced by the vibration; longer waves make a lower sound and shorter waves make a higher sound.

🎼 **Creating Music**: By carefully adjusting the water level in each glass, you can create different pitches to play a simple melody or tune.

Explore further

Fluid Symphony: Replace water in the glasses with other liquids like oil, syrup, or milk. Observe and record how the change in fluid affects the musical notes produced. Do heavier or more viscous fluids change the pitch or quality of the sound compared to lighter fluids?

Bottle Orchestra: Experiment using different types of bottles instead of glasses. Water bottles, soda bottles, or any other kind of container can be used. Tap on them to create sounds and compare the tones produced by bottles to those from glasses. Note the differences in pitch, volume, and resonance.

(6) Healthy Lungs

Take a deep breath and dive into understanding your body with the 'Healthy Lungs' activity! Your lungs are like balloons, filling with air when you breathe in. But just how much air can they hold? Everyone's lung capacity is different, an important indicator of respiratory health. In this experiment, you'll measure your lung capacity in a fun and simple way by using water displacement. Prepare to be amazed as you discover the power of your breath and learn more about how your lungs work!

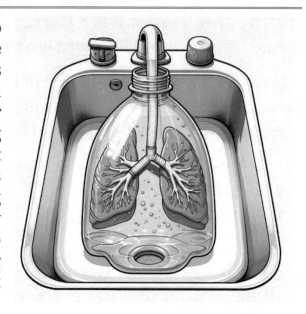

Material

+ Clean plastic tube
+ A plastic bottle
+ Tap water
+ Kitchen sink

Instructions

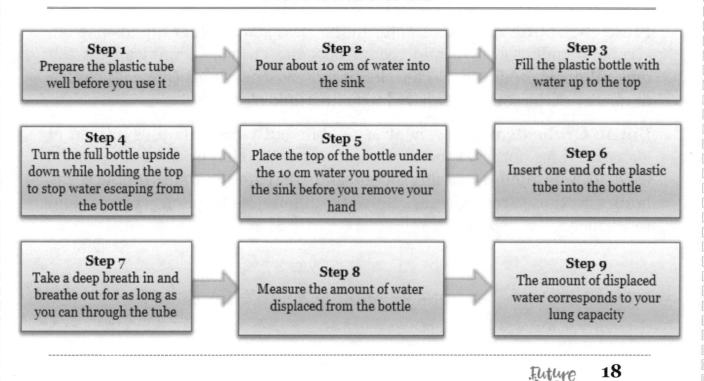

Step 1
Prepare the plastic tube well before you use it

Step 2
Pour about 10 cm of water into the sink

Step 3
Fill the plastic bottle with water up to the top

Step 4
Turn the full bottle upside down while holding the top to stop water escaping from the bottle

Step 5
Place the top of the bottle under the 10 cm water you poured in the sink before you remove your hand

Step 6
Insert one end of the plastic tube into the bottle

Step 7
Take a deep breath in and breathe out for as long as you can through the tube

Step 8
Measure the amount of water displaced from the bottle

Step 9
The amount of displaced water corresponds to your lung capacity

Science

Breath Out: When you exhale into the tube, air from your lungs travels through and enters the bottle, pushing water out.

Water Displacement: The air you breathe out displaces an equivalent volume of water from the bottle. This displacement allows you to measure the air volume you exhale, reflecting your lung capacity.

Measuring Volume: By measuring the amount of water pushed out, you can calculate the volume of air your lungs expelled. This is typically done by marking the water level before and after the experiment.

Lung Capacity & Oxygen Distribution: Lung capacity is an indicator of how much oxygen your lungs can distribute throughout your body. A higher lung capacity means more oxygen can be taken in and utilized by your body during activities.

Explore further

Lung Capacity Research:

Investigate the typical lung capacity ranges for different ages and genders. Compare your experimental results with these standards. Reflect on and implement ways to enhance the accuracy of your measurements, such as ensuring airtight connections or consistent breathing techniques.

Family & Friends Challenge: Invite family members and friends to participate in the experiment. Record each person's lung capacity and compile the data into a comparative table. Discuss any interesting patterns or differences you observe. Consider factors like age, fitness level, and height that might influence lung capacity.

(7) Secret Lemon Messages

Embark on a clandestine adventure with 'Secret Lemon Messages'! Uncover the ancient art of invisible writing using just a lemon and a few household items. In this thrilling activity, you'll learn how to craft secret notes that remain hidden to the eye until revealed by a special trick. Whether you're passing top-secret notes or just having fun with science, this experiment will show you the intriguing possibilities of natural acids and reveal the hidden messages waiting to be discovered. Grab a lemon and let's start our covert communication!

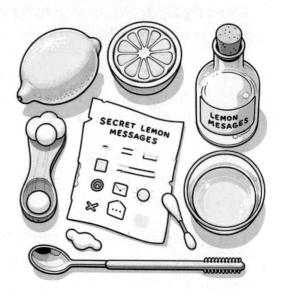

Material

+ Half a lemon
+ Tap water
+ spoon
+ Bowl
+ Cotton bud
+ White paper

Instructions

Step 1
Squeeze half lemon into a bowl and add a few drops of tap water

Step 2
Use a spoon to mix the lemon juice and the tap water in the bowl

Step 3
Dip the cotton bud into the lemon-water mixture

Step 4
Use the cotton bud as a pen and write your secrete text on a piece of paper

Step 5
Wait for your text to dry so it becomes completely invisible

Step 6
When you want to see your text, heat the paper by holding it close to a light bulb

Science

🌢 **Lemon Juice & Water**: Mixing lemon juice with water creates a near-invisible substance on paper. This diluted lemon juice is hard to detect once applied, making it perfect for secret messages.

🔍 **Invisible on Paper**: When you write on paper with this mixture, it dries clear. It appears blank to anyone looking at the paper, keeping your message hidden.

🌢 **Heat Causes Oxidation**: Lemon juice contains compounds that oxidize or chemically react with oxygen when heated. This oxidation process turns the juice (and your secret message) brown.

📄 **Revealing the Message**: Applying heat to the paper, such as with a light bulb, iron, or other heat sources, causes the lemon juice to change color and reveal your hidden writing.

🍎🧁 **Other Substances**: Not just lemon juice, but other organic substances like orange juice, honey, milk, vinegar, and wine can also work for invisible ink due to similar properties of oxidation when heated.

Explore further

Invisible Ink Variety

Test various substances as invisible inks, including orange juice, milk, honey, vinegar, and wine. Apply each to paper, let it dry, and then heat it to reveal the message. Note which substance provides the clearest, most readable text when revealed.

Revelation Techniques

Discover different methods to bring your hidden messages to light. Instead of using a light bulb's heat, try an iron, hair dryer, or even sunlight. Observe and record each method's effectiveness and differences in revealing the secret text.

(8) Test your Dominant Side

Embark on a journey of self-discovery with 'Test Your Dominant Side'! This experiment is a fun and interactive way to understand the amazing teamwork between your brain and body. Through a series of engaging activities, you'll uncover which side of your body tends to take the lead - be it your left or right. By the end of this adventure, you'll have a deeper insight into how your brain coordinates your movements and preferences. Get ready to explore the dominant aspects of your eyes, hands, and legs, and learn a little more about yourself!

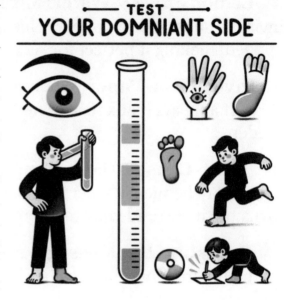

Material

+ A cup of water
+ An empty tube
+ A small ball
+ A paper or a notebook
+ A pen

Instructions

Perform the following tests and check the box under the right column (left or right):

Test		Left	Right
(1)	**Eye tests**		
	(1.1) Which eye do you use to wink?		
	(1.2) Look into an empty tube (like an old paper towel tube); which eye did you use?		

Test	Left	Right
(1.3) Make a triangle shape using your fingers and thumbs, and bring your hands together to make the triangle smaller. Look into the hole between your hands and find a small object in your room to focus on using both eyes. Now try to close your left eye and then your right eye. Did the view of the object change when you closed your left or right eye?		
(2) Hand and arm test		
(2.1) When you write, which hand do you use?		
(2.2) Which hand do you use to pick up a cup of water?		
(2.3) Throw a ball. Which arm did you use?		
(3) Foot and leg tests		
(3.1) Run forward and jump off one leg. Which leg did you use to jump off?		
(3.2) Place the ball on the floor and kick it. Which foot did you use?		

Science

The human brain is a complicated organ that has been under study by many disciplines, such as psychology, neurology, physics, and sociology. However, many undiscovered processes remain due to almost 100 billion neurons and 100 trillion connections hidden inside the brain. The right and left hemispheres are one of the most important discoveries in the last centuries.

The main difference between these two hemispheres is the abilities they provide to a person in their dominance. For example, if you enjoy music, art classes, and social studies, there is a big chance that the right hemisphere of your brain is dominant. On the contrary, if you enjoy maths, science, and logical challenges, your left brain hemisphere is most likely the dominant one.

So, what side do you favour? Are you left or right-handed? Are you left or right-footed? Do you use your left or right eye? Studies revealed that around 90% of people are right-handed. While the reason behind that is unclear, the cause is believed to be related to the side of the brain people use for language. The right side of the body is controlled by the left hemisphere of the brain, which controls language in 90% of people. Some scientists believe the reason behind the right-hand dominance is related to culture since the word right is associated with doing the right thing, whereas the left is connected to doing something wrong or weak.

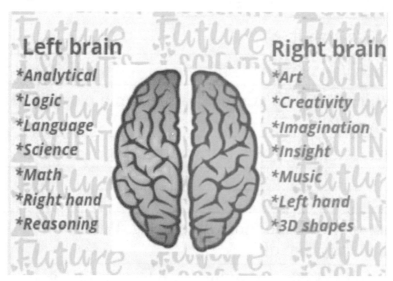

What does it mean if you are left-brain dominant?

If you are left-brain dominant, you are a more analytical/logical person. Some fields for a left-brain person include:

- Business
- Programming
- Engineering
- Reporting
- Science
- Finance

Left-brain dominant persons would benefit from the following tips:

➢ Study in a quiet room and avoid distractions
➢ Do more volunteer work
➢ Participate in science fairs or math competitions
➢ Read more non-fiction books
➢ If you are to choose a task in an assignment, try to side with analytical essays instead of creative writing.

What does it mean if you are right-brain dominant?

You are a more creative/artistic person if you are right-brain dominant. Some fields for a right-brain person include:

- Graphic design
- Music
- Counselling
- Paint
- Psychology
- Management

Right-brain dominant persons would benefit from the following tips:

➢ Choose to write personal essays
➢ Find a hobby you like and practice it
➢ Use your creativity when writing and expand on your writing language
➢ Use more images and charts when you study
➢ Help yourself to remember directions by writing them down
➢ Don't let yourself get distracted when you listen; practice mindful listening

Explore further

👀 Extended Eye Tests

Beyond looking through a tube, try reading text or catching a ball with one eye covered, then switch eyes. Observe which eye seems to provide better coordination and clarity. This can further indicate your dominant eye.

🤝 Ambidexterity Training

Practice doing everyday activities with your non-dominant hand, like brushing your teeth, eating, or even drawing. Keep a progress diary over a week or more to see if you improve and how it affects your hand dominance.

🔍 Family & Friends Survey

Conduct the same series of tests with family members or friends. Compare results to see the variety of dominant sides within your group. Discuss how dominance might affect abilities or preferences in sports, writing, or other activities.

Fun Facts: Human Brain

Your brain allows us to think, analyze, store memories, and make decisions. At the same time, it controls other areas in our bodies, such as nerves and breathing. The human brain's average weight is 3 pounds, which is around 2% of total body weight. Our brain consists of three main parts: the Cerebrum, the Cerebellum, and the Brainstem.

The Cerebrum: This is the largest part of the brain and is responsible for speech, motion, movement, and learning.

The Cerebellum: This part is located under the Cerebrum. It is responsible for balance, muscle movements, and body posture.

The Brainstem: Connects the spinal cord to the Cerebrum and Cerebellum. It looks after several body functions, such as temperature, digestion, and heart rate.

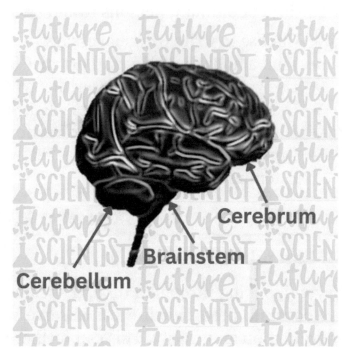

The Cerebrum

Brainstem

Cerebellum

The Cerebrum is split into two parts: the left and right hemispheres. The **left hemisphere** controls the **right side of your body**, and the **right hemisphere** controls the **left side of your body**. The left hemisphere is very good with analytical and verbal tasks, whereas the right hemisphere is very good at reading, writing, and music.

🗨 **Brain Power**: The human brain is the body's command center, orchestrating thoughts, memory, movement, and emotions. Despite its power, it's soft and squishy, similar in consistency to soft tofu or gelatin.

⚡ **Electric Brain**: Your brain is a supercharged network with about 100 billion neurons. These neurons fire and communicate through electrical impulses, making thousands of connections and creating thoughts, memories, and movements.

Starlight, Star Brain: If all the neurons in your brain were to light up, they would generate enough electricity to power a low-wattage bulb. Your brain's activity and energy make it a small but mighty powerhouse!

Unconscious Genius: Even when you're sleeping, your brain is busy. It's working on consolidating memories, solving problems, and cleaning up waste from neural activity. It's like a night shift worker that never takes a break.

Detective Brain: The brain is incredibly good at recognizing faces. You can recognize hundreds or even thousands of different faces, often noticing them in a fraction of a second!

Learning Machine: Your brain has a fantastic ability to adapt and rewire itself. Learning new skills, languages, or even recovering from injuries involves the brain making new neural connections, a process known as neuroplasticity.

Most Energy-Intensive Organ: Despite being only about 2% of your body's weight, your brain uses around 20% of your energy intake. It's a real energy hog, needing constant fuel to support its complex tasks.

Language Powerhouse: The left hemisphere of the brain is typically responsible for language skills. If damaged early in life, the right hemisphere can often adapt to take over these language functions, showcasing the brain's adaptability.

Imagination and Dreams: The brain's occipital lobe helps you understand and interpret images and visuals. It's active when imagining things and when you're dreaming, painting vivid pictures from your thoughts and memories.

Happy Chemicals: Your brain releases chemicals affecting your mood and emotions. For instance, dopamine is the "feel-good" neurotransmitter, which plays a crucial role in pleasure and motivation.

Social Network: Your brain has specific areas dedicated to understanding and interacting with others. This social brain helps you empathize, communicate, and build complex social networks unique to humans.

(9) Bubbling Citrus Blast

Embark on a bubbly adventure with 'Bubbling Citrus Blast'! Across the globe, sodas sparkle with their irresistible fizz. Ever wonder what makes them dance with bubbles? Dive into the fizzy world by creating your very own sparkling citrus drink right at home. With a few simple ingredients, you'll unlock the secret behind the bubbles and whip up a refreshing concoction that's all yours. So squeeze those lemons, add a dash of fizz, and prepare to sip on science with every gulp!

Material

- Two lemons
- Cold water
- 1 teaspoon of baking soda
- 1 teaspoon of sugar
- A cup
- Lemon juicer

Instructions

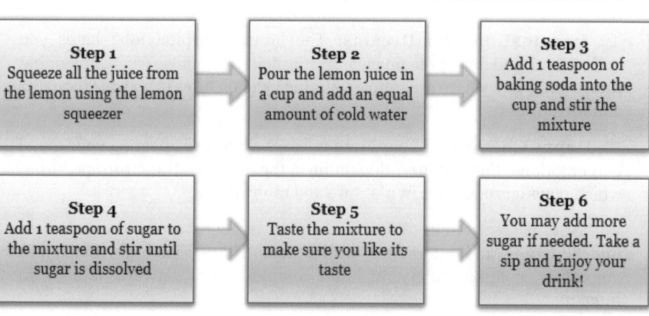

Step 1
Squeeze all the juice from the lemon using the lemon squeezer

Step 2
Pour the lemon juice in a cup and add an equal amount of cold water

Step 3
Add 1 teaspoon of baking soda into the cup and stir the mixture

Step 4
Add 1 teaspoon of sugar to the mixture and stir until sugar is dissolved

Step 5
Taste the mixture to make sure you like its taste

Step 6
You may add more sugar if needed. Take a sip and Enjoy your drink!

Science

Lemon Juice: The main ingredient, lemon juice, is acidic. It's the sour, tangy liquid we use to give the drink its distinctive taste.

Baking Soda: Baking soda, or sodium bicarbonate, is a base. When it's added to the acidic lemon juice, it neutralizes some of the acid.

Acid-Base Reaction: The interaction between the acidic lemon juice and the basic baking soda creates a chemical reaction. This reaction produces carbon dioxide (CO_2) gas, which forms the bubbles you see.

Fizzy Creation: These bubbles of CO_2 give the drink its fizzy, sparkling quality. It's the same type of carbonation found in commercial sodas and sparkling beverages.

Taste Transformation: The result is a fizzy drink that not only tickles your taste buds with its effervescence but also has the tangy flavor of lemonade, transforming a simple juice into a sparkling treat.

Explore further

Juice Variations

Experiment with different types of juices such as orange, grapefruit, or lime in place of lemon juice. Observe and note the differences in taste, fizziness, and reaction speed with the baking soda. Each juice's unique acidity will affect the reaction and flavor of the fizzy drink.

Temperature Test

Try the experiment with water at various temperatures. Use ice-cold water, room temperature water, and warm water to see how temperature affects the rate and intensity of the fizzing reaction. Record any noticeable differences in how quickly or vigorously the baking soda reacts with the lemon juice.

(10) Soda Geyser Spectacle

Get ready to witness the explosive 'Soda Geyser Spectacle'! This thrilling outdoor experiment combines Diet Coke and Mentos to create an astonishing eruption. Unlike many other reactions you see in science, this one is all about physics, not chemistry. As the Mentos dive into the soda, a spectacular geyser of fizz rockets skyward! It's a fascinating and fun way to explore the principles of nucleation and pressure. So, gather your materials, step outside, and prepare to be amazed by your fizzy fountain!

Material

- 1 large bottle of Diet Coke
- ½ bag of Mentos
- Optional geyser tube

Instructions

Step 1 Find a proper outdoor spot to perform this experiment	**Step 2** Hold the Diet Coke bottle upright and unscrew the lid	**Step 3** Drop half pack of Mentos in the Diet Coke bottle using geyser tube if available
Step 4 Quickly step back from the Diet Coke bottle without tipping the bottle or disturbing the reaction	**Step 5** Watch the eruption and record its height and for how long it lasts	**Step 6** Clean up any parts of the house that were splashed by the Diet Coke eruption

Science

Carbonated Soda: Diet Coke and other sodas are carbonated, meaning they contain dissolved carbon dioxide (CO_2) gas. This CO_2 is what gives sodas their fizz and pop.

Pressurized Bottle: The CO_2 in the soda is under pressure in the sealed bottle. When you open the bottle, the gas begins to escape, creating bubbles, especially when poured.

Mentos Effect: Dropping Mentos into the bottle causes a rapid release of CO_2. The candy doesn't cause a chemical reaction but provides a surface for the CO_2 to form bubbles rapidly.

Surface Tension & Dimples: The Mentos candies have a rough, dimpled surface. These tiny dimples drastically increase the candy's surface area, breaking the liquid's surface tension and allowing more bubbles to form quickly.

Geyser Eruption: As bubbles form rapidly on the Mentos, they push the liquid up and out of the bottle in a spectacular geyser-like eruption, showcasing a physical reaction between the surface of the candies and the soda.

Explore further

Crushed Mentos Test

Try the experiment using Mentos crushed into smaller pieces rather than whole candies. Observe and record the difference in the eruption's intensity and height. Reflect on how the change in surface area of the Mentos affects the reaction.

Soda Age Comparison

Conduct the experiment using an older bottle of Diet Coke and compare the results with a newer, fresher bottle. Note any differences in the geyser's height or the speed of the reaction. Discuss the possible reasons for any variations, considering factors like CO_2 loss over time.

(11) Gravity-Defying Water

Prepare to defy gravity with the 'Gravity-Defying Water' experiment! Discover the invisible might of air pressure in this simple yet astonishing activity. You'll fill a glass with water, seal it with a card, and then bravely turn it upside down. Watch in amazement as the water stays put, seemingly defying gravity! This experiment will help you explore the balancing forces of air pressure and gravity, demonstrating that sometimes what goes up doesn't always come down. Get ready to challenge what you know about holding water!

Material

+ A glass of water
+ A sink

+ An index card or a piece of construction paper

Instructions

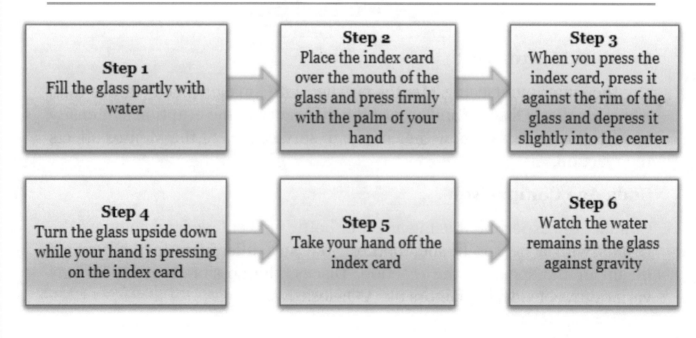

Step 1
Fill the glass partly with water

Step 2
Place the index card over the mouth of the glass and press firmly with the palm of your hand

Step 3
When you press the index card, press it against the rim of the glass and depress it slightly into the center

Step 4
Turn the glass upside down while your hand is pressing on the index card

Step 5
Take your hand off the index card

Step 6
Watch the water remains in the glass against gravity

Science

▽ **Downward Water Pressure**: The water in the glass exerts a downward force on the card due to gravity, trying to push the card away and spill out.

△ **Upward Air Pressure**: Simultaneously, air pressure from the environment pushes up against the card. This is the force of the air molecules colliding with the card's surface.

⚖ **Balancing Forces**: When the upward air pressure matches the downward pressure of the water, the forces balance out. This equilibrium keeps the card in place, preventing the water from spilling.

⬅ **Trial and Variation**: Achieving this balance might require some trial and error. Experimenting with different sizes of index cards or varying water amounts can help find the right balance where the forces equalize, effectively demonstrating the principle.

Explore further

Glass Shape Variation

Experiment with glasses of different shapes and sizes. Observe whether the shape or size of the glass affects the ability to keep the water inside when turned upside down. Record which shapes seem to hold the card and water most effectively.

Water Level Adjustments

Alter the amount of water in the glass for each trial. Start with just a little water and gradually increase the amount each time. Note the water level at which the experiment works best and any changes in the balance of forces.

Card Material Test

Try the experiment using different materials for the card, such as plastic, cardboard, or even fabric. Note how each material interacts with the water and air pressure. Does a stiffer card hold the water better, or does a more flexible one work best? Record the differences in effectiveness and any interesting observations.

(12) Homemade String Symphony

Strum into the ancient and enchanting world of guitars with our 'Homemade String Symphony' activity! Guitars have serenaded audiences for over 4,000 years, evolving from simple strings to the modern marvels we know today. In this creative endeavor, you'll craft your very own guitar using everyday materials. Discover the science of sound and vibration as you assemble rubber bands, a tissue box, and a paper towel tube into a delightful instrument. It's time to make music history in your own home!

Material

+ 4 rubber bands of the same length and varying thickness
+ Glue
+ Packing tape
+ Empty tissue box
+ Empty paper towel tube
+ Two large craft sticks
+ Scissors

Instructions

Step 1
Remove any plastic from inside the tissue box

Step 2
Attach the paper towel tube to one short end of the tissue box using tape. The tube should align with the tissue box opening

Step 3
Glue a craft stick to the two edges of the tissue box opening. The sticks should be perpendicular to the opening direction

Step 4
When the glue dries, wrap the 4 rubber bands around the tissue box such that they rest on the craft sticks

Step 5
Hold the guitar by the paper towel tube and pluck the rubber bands. Check which band makes a higher pitch sound

Step 6
Press your figure down on each band such that the band is pinched between your finger and the craft stick. Notice the sound changes when the rubber band is pressed

Science

🎸 **Rubber Band Strings**: When you pluck the rubber bands stretched across your homemade guitar, they vibrate, producing sound. This mimics how real guitar strings work.

🎶 **Vibration Equals Sound**: The sound you hear is due to the vibration of the rubber bands. The faster the vibration, the sound waves it creates, and the more the air around them vibrates, transmitting sound to your ears.

👆 **Pitch and Thickness**: The thickness of each rubber band affects the pitch of the sound. Thinner bands vibrate more quickly and produce higher-pitched sounds, while thicker bands vibrate slower and create lower-pitched sounds.

🎵 **Sound Variation**: Experimenting with different thicknesses and lengths of rubber bands will change the sound your homemade guitar makes, allowing you to create a variety of tones and pitches.

Explore further

Tissue Box Variations: Experiment with tissue boxes of different sizes or modify the opening of a single box. Observe how changing the size or shape of the box's opening affects the pitch and quality of the sound produced by the rubber band strings. Record the differences in sound with each variation.

Thickness and Pitch: Use sets of rubber bands with varying thicknesses. Test how each thickness affects the pitch of the sound when plucked. Notice whether the thicker bands produce lower sounds compared to the thinner ones and how the tension affects the vibrations.

Length and Tension: Adjust the length and tension of the rubber bands by stretching them more or less across the box. Observe how these changes impact the pitch and volume of the sound. Does a tighter band produce a higher or louder note?

Fun Facts: Sound Waves

Sound is the movement of energy through particles in a wave-like pattern. Three elements are essential to create and experience sound: **a source, a receiver, and a medium**. The source, like a musical instrument, generates the sound. The receiver, such as our ears or a microphone, captures and interprets the sound. The medium, usually air, is what the sound waves travel through. These waves are the energy vibrations moving from the source to the receiver, bringing sounds to life.

Our ears catch every sound we hear as tiny vibrations. Our ears are complex structures with three main parts: the outer ear, the middle ear, and the inner ear.

The outer ear, which you can see, includes the ear canal that captures sound waves and funnels them to the eardrum.

The middle ear, located just inside the eardrum, contains air and tiny bones that help transmit the vibrations to the inner ear.

The inner ear is a fluid-filled chamber where vibrations move tiny hair cells. These hair cells then create signals sent to the auditory nerve, leading to the brain, which interprets the sounds. While our ears collect the sounds, the brain does the heavy lifting in sorting and understanding what we hear."

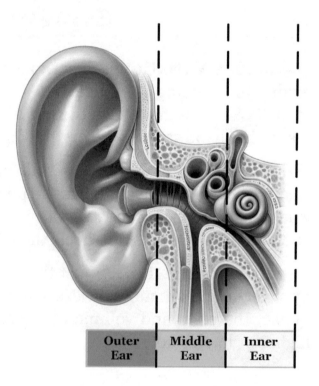

Outer Ear | Middle Ear | Inner Ear

💭 **Light vs. Sound**: Light zips through space at 186,000 miles per second, while sound ambles at about 770 miles per hour. That's why we see lightning before we hear thunder - light reaches us much faster than sound!

📢 **Decibels and Hearing**: Sounds are measured in decibels (dB). Normal conversation hovers around 60 dB, but sounds above 85 dB can harm our ears. Concerts can reach up to 130 dB, blasting past the safe threshold.

🌌 **Sound in Space**: Sound needs particles to travel, bouncing off them to move. Space is a vacuum with no particles, so sound can't travel there. Space is eerily silent!

🐶 **Dogs and Frequency**: Dogs have an amazing hearing range and can detect sounds at much higher frequencies than humans, allowing them to hear things that we cannot.

👂 **Ear Size and Hearing**: Generally, animals with larger ears have a better hearing capacity, as bigger ears can capture more sound waves. On the other hand, some insects, like flies, don't rely on hearing at all!

💧 **Speed in Water**: Sound waves travel around four times faster in water than in air, which is why sounds under the sea can be heard over longer distances more quickly.

🎹 **Musical Octaves**: Human hearing typically ranges from 20 Hz to 20,000 Hz. Musical notes double in frequency every octave, giving us a wide variety of pitches to enjoy in music and life.

🐋 **Whale Communication**: Whales use low-frequency sound waves to communicate over vast distances in the ocean. These sounds can travel for hundreds, even thousands, of miles underwater.

👂 **Echolocation**: Bats and dolphins use echolocation to navigate and hunt. They emit high-frequency sounds that bounce off objects and return, helping them "see" their environment through sound.

(13) Blast Off Bottle Rocket

Embark on an exciting journey into the basics of rocket science! You can create your own rocket using just a few everyday items like a plastic bottle, water, a cork, and an air pump. The secret lies in pumping air inside the bottle until it propels like a rocket. This hands-on experiment is a thrilling way to explore the principles of propulsion and aerodynamics. So, gather your materials, strap your safety gear, and prepare for a spectacular liftoff!

Material

- An empty plastic bottle, such as 1 or 2-liter pop bottle
- A cork that fits perfectly into the bottle opening
- Protective gloves and safety goggles
- Scissors
- Water
- 2 large foam blocks (10 cm think)

- A bike air pump with a hose and pump needle
- A drill with a bit around the same size as the pump needle
- Thick cardboard
- Thin cardboard
- Duct tape
- 2 wooden blocks or bricks

Instructions

Step 1
Find a proper open outdoor space with nothing overhead to perform this activity

Step 2
Insert the cork into the top of the plastic bottle. Make sure it fits tight. If the cork is small, line it with duct tape to make it larger

Step 3
Wear your protective gloves and safety goggles.

Step 4
Drill a hole through the center of the cork from top to bottom. Make sure that the drill pit the same size of the air pump needle. You may need an adult assistant for this step

Step 5
Insert the pump needle through the hole until it is secure. Make sure that the needle fits tightly into the hole

Step 6
To test the tightness, remove the cork and add water into the bottle and reseal it with the cork while the needle still in place. Flip the bottle and check for any leakage. Use the duct tape to fix any leak

Step 7
Use the thick cardboard to cut 3 equal triangles. Use these triangles to create fins for your rocket. Cover the triangles with duct tape to protect them from water

Step 8
Tape the fins to the flat part of the plastic bottle near its nozzle. The top part of the bottle represents the bottom of your rocket, so position the flat side of your fins downward to support the bottle when it stands upside down

Step 9
Use the thin cardboard to cut a piece that acts as the nose of your rocket. Attach the piece to the bottom of the bottle, which represents the top of your rocket

Step 10
Use 2 wooden blocks, or 2 bricks, to create a launch pad for your rocket. Place the blocks 3 cm apart to position the bottle nose between them

Step 11
Remove the cork with the pump needle still in place. Add water to the bottle until it is less than ½ full (about 40% full). Reinsert the cork into the bottle rocket and make sure no water leaks out. Use the duct tape to fix any leak

Step 12
Move away from the rocket and use the bicycle pump to pump air into the bottle. Once the air pressure is high enough, the cork will pop out and the rocket will launch into the air. Stay away from the rocket

Illustrations

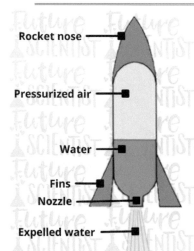

- Rocket nose
- Pressurized air
- Water
- Fins
- Nozzle
- Expelled water

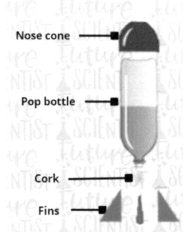

- Nose cone
- Pop bottle
- Cork
- Fins

Science

Newton's laws of motion explain the motion of the water bottle rocket:

Newton's 1st law of motion

This law states that an **object will remain at rest unless an unbalanced force acts upon it.** In our case, the bottle rocket remains at rest until the force from the air pumped by the bicycle pump acts upon it.

Newton's 2nd law of motion

The law describes the relationship between **force, acceleration,** and **mass**. In our case, the amount of force pushing the bottle rocket upwards depends on the volume of air pumped into the rocket. When you add water to the bottle, the water increases the rocket's mass, which increases the action force applied as the water is expelled by the air pumped into the rocket. This process caused the rocket to accelerate upwards faster.

Newton's 3rd law of motion

This law states that **every action has an equal and opposite reaction**. In our case, the force created by the water and air being expelled downwards out of the bottle was the action force; the reaction force was the bottle being pushed upwards.

Four forces are acting on the bottle rocket when it is launched:

1. **Weight**: a downward-acting force generated by the Earth's gravity.
2. **Thrust**: a force in the direction of motion generated by the rocket propulsion system, based on Newton's 3rd law of motion.
3. **Lift**: a force which acts perpendicular to the direction of motion.
4. **Drag**: a force that acts opposite to the direction of motion.

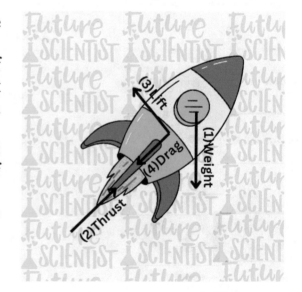

As you pump air into the bottle, the pressure inside builds up; this air pressure pushes out in all directions, including downwards on the cork. At a specific air pressure level, the friction between the cork and the bottle is not enough to hold the cork; at this point, the cork is pushed out. Consequently, the water is pushed out by the air you have pumped in. This means that the main factor controlling what pressure the rocket launches at and how high it goes is the amount of friction on the cork. As the water is pushed out, the air expands, and air pressure decreases. Eventually, after approximately 2-3 minutes, the rocket runs out of water, coasting for the rest of its journey.

Explore further

Varying Bottle Sizes: Use soda bottles of different capacities and compare how each size influences the rocket's launch height. Document the effect of bottle size on the rocket's performance.

Fin Shapes and Flight: Attach fins of various geometric shapes to your rockets. Test how shapes like triangles, rectangles, or circles affect the rocket's ascent and stability.

Balancing Act: Experiment with adding different weights to the rocket. Observe how the placement and amount of weight change the flight pattern and peak altitude.

Nozzle Dynamics: Modify the nozzle diameter at the bottom of the rocket. Analyze the impact of nozzle size on the launch velocity and maximum height reached.

Launch Angle Exploration: Alter the angle from which you launch the rocket. Record the differences in flight trajectory and determine the optimal angle for the highest or longest flight.

Fun Facts: Rocket Science

📄 **Ancient Fire Arrows**: Did you know? The earliest rockets were made in China over 1,000 years ago, and they were like fire arrows powered by gunpowder!

▨ **Zooming to Space**: To break free from Earth's gravity, rockets need to hit the "escape velocity" of 25,000 miles per hour—that's like circling the entire Earth in about an hour!

🌑 **Giant Leap**: The Saturn V was the towering rocket that carried astronauts to the moon. It was as tall as a 36-story skyscraper!

🛰 **Space Messengers**: We've sent spacecraft to every planet in our solar system, thanks to rockets. The Voyager probes even carry a golden record with sounds and images from Earth.

♻ **Eco-Friendly Rockets**: Nowadays, rockets can come back home! Companies are designing rockets that can be reused for multiple trips to space.

✳ **Rocket Recipes**: Rocket fuel isn't just gas—it's a mix, including an oxidizer, which is a chemical that allows fuel to burn in space where there's no air.

💧 **Vacuum-Proof Flames**: Rocket engines can burn fuel in space's vacuum by carrying their oxygen supply, letting them create thrust anywhere!

Satellite Launch: Satellites, our space helpers, reach their orbit by catching a ride on a rocket. They come in all sizes, from tiny cubes to as big as a bus.

Space Gardening: We've sent seeds to space in rockets to see how they grow in zero gravity, teaching us about life's potential beyond Earth.

Tough Materials: Rockets are built with super materials that can handle the hot blasts of launch and the icy chill of space without breaking a sweat.

Speedy Rockets: The fastest rocket is the New Horizons probe. It zoomed off Earth at a whopping 36,000 miles per hour to visit Pluto and beyond.

Space Animals: Animals were the first astronauts! Laika, a brave dog, was the first to orbit Earth in a spacecraft, paving the way for human space travel.

Stages of a Rocket: Rockets often have multiple parts, called stages. Each stage has its own engine and fuel, and they fall off as the fuel is used up, helping the rocket go faster and further.

NASA's Rocket Garden: At NASA's Kennedy Space Center, there's a special place called the Rocket Garden. Here, you can see real rockets from space missions, just like a museum of space history!

(14) Super Sugar Bubbles

Dive into the enchanting world of bubble science with 'Super Sugar Bubbles'! This experiment isn't just about creating bubbles; it's about making them stronger and bouncier. By mixing everyday ingredients like water, dish soap, and a secret component – sugar – you'll create a bubble solution that makes more resilient bubbles. Watch as these bubbles bounce on your gloved hands! Grab a bubble wand and a bowl, and explore the fascinating science that makes bubbles more durable and delightful!

Material

- 4 tablespoon tap water
- 1 tablespoon liquid dishwashing soap
- 2 tablespoon sugar
- Soft knit gloves
- Bubble wand, such as a slotted spatula
- Small bowl

Instructions

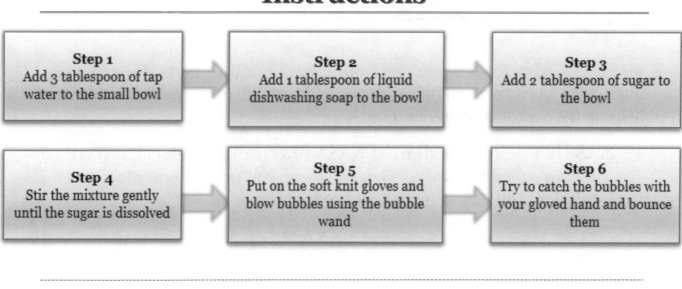

Step 1
Add 3 tablespoon of tap water to the small bowl

Step 2
Add 1 tablespoon of liquid dishwashing soap to the bowl

Step 3
Add 2 tablespoon of sugar to the bowl

Step 4
Stir the mixture gently until the sugar is dissolved

Step 5
Put on the soft knit gloves and blow bubbles using the bubble wand

Step 6
Try to catch the bubbles with your gloved hand and bounce them

Science

● **Bubble Structure**: A bubble is a pocket of air caught in a soap film. This film consists of four thin layers: two layers of soap sandwiching layers of water and sugar.

💧 **Layers in Action**: These layers work together to trap air, forming a bubble. The outer and inner soap layers help maintain the bubble's shape, while the water layer provides flexibility.

🍃 **Sugar's Role**: Sugar in the bubble solution slows down the evaporation of water. This reduced evaporation helps the bubbles last longer before popping.

☁ **Evaporation and Popping**: Bubbles pop when the water between the layers evaporates, causing the soap film to become too thin to stay intact.

👐 **Hand Oils and Bubbles**: The natural oils on our hands can break the surface tension of the bubble film, leading to a pop. This is why touching bubbles usually bursts them.

✊ **Gloved Protection**: Wearing soft winter gloves protects the bubbles from direct contact with hand oils. This allows the bubbles to last longer and even bounce without popping.

Explore further

Soap Quantity Test: Experiment with varying amounts of dishwashing soap in your bubble mixture. Observe how the size and lifespan of the bubbles change with different soap concentrations. Record the relationship between the amount of soap and bubble characteristics.

No Sugar Challenge: Try making bubbles without adding sugar. Compare the stability and longevity of these bubbles to those with sugar. Analyze the differences in popping time and hypothesize why sugar affects bubble longevity.

Temperature Experiment: Conduct the experiment in different temperatures—indoors, outdoors, in a cooler environment. Note how temperature affects bubble formation, size, and lifespan.

(15) Frosty Flavor: Homemade Ice Cream

Welcome to the sweet and chilly world of 'Frosty Flavor: Homemade Ice Cream'! Who says you need an ice cream machine to whip up a delicious frozen treat? In this experiment, you'll learn how to make your own ice cream right at home using simple ingredients and a bit of science magic. Add your favorite flavors, from classic chocolate syrup to crunchy Oreo bits, and watch as cream transforms into ice cream before your eyes. Grab your ingredients and get ready to shake up some science—and satisfy your sweet tooth!

Material

- 1 cup of half & half cream
- 2 tablespoons of sugar
- ½ tablespoon of vanilla extract
- 3 cubes of ice
- 1/3 cup of rock salt
- 1 small sealable plastic bag
- A big sealable plastic bag
- Small bowl
- Your preferred toppings, such as chocolate syrup, Oreos, etc.

Instructions

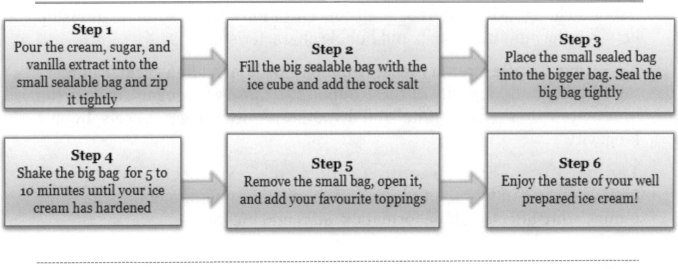

Step 1
Pour the cream, sugar, and vanilla extract into the small sealable bag and zip it tightly

Step 2
Fill the big sealable bag with the ice cube and add the rock salt

Step 3
Place the small sealed bag into the bigger bag. Seal the big bag tightly

Step 4
Shake the big bag for 5 to 10 minutes until your ice cream has hardened

Step 5
Remove the small bag, open it, and add your favourite toppings

Step 6
Enjoy the taste of your well prepared ice cream!

Science

💧 **Quick Chill**: The key to making ice cream is rapidly cooling the ingredients. Ice cubes help swiftly lower the temperature of the ice cream mixture.

Salt's Magic: Adding salt to ice changes the game. Salt lowers the freezing point of water, making the ice-salt mixture even colder than ice alone.

❄ **Colder Than Ice**: As the ice melts, the salty water becomes colder than plain ice water. This super-cold mixture is crucial for the ice cream-making process.

💧 ➡ ♨ **Heat Transfer**: When the ice-salt mixture sloshes around the ice cream ingredients in the bag, it absorbs heat from the ingredients. This process of heat transfer is what transforms the mixture into ice cream.

⏱ **Speedy Transformation**: The combination of the cold mixture and continuous movement turns the liquid ingredients into the familiar texture of ice cream in just minutes.

Explore further

Varying Salt Levels

Test the effect of different salt quantities on your ice cream. Does more salt make the ice cream form faster? Record the time it takes for the ice cream to freeze with varying salt amounts.

Salt-Free Experiment

Make a batch of ice cream without salt. Compare the freezing time and texture with the batch made using the salt-ice mixture. How does the absence of salt affect the process?

Different Liquid Bases

Experiment with different liquid bases, like whole milk, cream, or a milk substitute. Observe how each base influences the taste and texture of the ice cream.

(16) Flame Symphony

Step into the mesmerizing world of sound and light with the 'Flame Symphony' experiment! Discover how music can visually come to life by making a candle flame dance to the beat. Simply place a candle between a pair of speakers and play your favorite tunes. As the music plays, watch in wonder as the flame sways and flickers in response to the vibrations. Adjust the volume and experiment with different songs to see how the flame reacts. It's fascinating to see the invisible power of sound waves and vibration in action!

Material

+ A candle
+ A candle holder

+ Two speakers, such as computer speakers or two smartphones.

Instructions

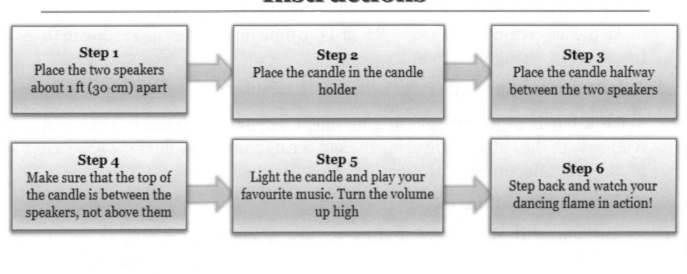

Step 1
Place the two speakers about 1 ft (30 cm) apart

Step 2
Place the candle in the candle holder

Step 3
Place the candle halfway between the two speakers

Step 4
Make sure that the top of the candle is between the speakers, not above them

Step 5
Light the candle and play your favourite music. Turn the volume up high

Step 6
Step back and watch your dancing flame in action!

Science

♫ **Music as Air Pressure Waves**: When music plays, it creates air pressure waves. These waves are initially electrical signals that get amplified and turned into vibrations by your speakers.

🔊 **Speaker Vibrations**: The amplifiers in the speakers vibrate in response to the music's electrical signals, recreating the sound as waves in the air.

🕯 **Flame Dance**: These air pressure waves travel from the speakers and hit the candle flame. The impact of these waves causes the flame to vibrate and 'dance' in response to the music.

👂 **Human Ear and Sound**: Similarly, when air pressure waves enter our ears, they strike the eardrum, a thin membrane, causing it to vibrate.

🌀 **From Vibration to Sound**: These vibrations are transmitted through the middle and inner ear. Our ears convert these vibrations into sounds that our brain can recognize and understand.

Explore further

Volume Variations: Adjust the volume on the speakers and watch the candle flame's reaction. Does a louder volume make the flame dance more vigorously? Record the flame's movement at different volume levels.

Speech vs. Music: Play a spoken word recording instead of music. Observe if the flame reacts differently to speech compared to music. Note the differences in flame movement with varying sound types.

Genre Effects: Experiment with different music genres – classical, rock, pop, etc. Does the flame respond differently to varying rhythms and beats?

Sound Frequency Test: Try playing sounds at different frequencies, from low bass to high treble. See how the frequency of the sound affects the flame's behavior.

(17) Eternal Fall: Leaf Preservation

Embrace fall's vibrant beauty with 'Eternal Fall: Leaf Preservation'! Fall leaves are fleeting treasures, their bright colors fading as they become homes for bacteria and fungi. In this activity, you'll learn how to capture and preserve the splendor of fall leaves for years to come. Not only will you create lasting natural art, but you'll also delve into the science behind why leaves change color each season. Gather some colorful leaves, wax paper, and an iron, and prepare to preserve a piece of autumn's magic!

Material

- An ironing board
- An iron
- Wax paper
- A collection of colourful leaves
- Scissors
- 2 towels

Instructions

Step 1
Place a towel on the ironing board

Step 2
Place a wax paper on top of the towel

Step 3
Place your leaves on the wax paper. Leave space between the leaves

Step 4
Cover the leaves with a second wax paper, parallel to the first one

Step 5
Place a second towel on the top of the second wax paper

Step 6
Ask for an adult help to set your iron at medium temperature

Step 7
When the iron is heated, run it over the second towel to seal the wax papers around your leaves

Step 8
Keep ironing for a few minutes until the wax papers have sealed perfectly on your leaves

Step 9
Turn off the iron and allow a few minutes for the leaves to cool down

Science

Leaf Life Cycle: Leaves get water from their tree through their stems. Once they fall, they no longer receive water, causing them to dry out and become brittle.

Moisture Loss: The fallen leaves lose their moisture quickly, which is why they don't stay vibrant for long after detaching from the tree.

Wax Preservation: Applying wax paper and heat to the leaves creates a protective hydrocarbon layer around them.

Hydrocarbon Barrier: This layer effectively seals the leaves' remaining moisture, preserving their color and flexibility.

Long-Lasting Beauty: Thanks to this preservation process, the leaves maintain their bright, fresh appearance for much longer than if left untreated.

Explore further

Window Light Display: Once your preserved leaves have cooled, hang the wax paper sheets on a window. Observe how the light filters through the leaves and note any color changes. Try to identify each leaf's tree species by its shape and color.

Leaf Comparison: Collect and preserve leaves from different types of trees. Compare their shapes, textures, and how they change over time after preservation. Create a leaf guide based on your observations.

Art with Leaves: Use your preserved leaves to create art. Arrange them in patterns or use them in a collage. Notice how the waxed leaves differ in texture and handling compared to fresh leaves.

Seasonal Study: Preserve leaves from different seasons. Compare the colors and conditions of spring, summer, and fall leaves. Document how leaf characteristics vary throughout the year.

(18) Soaring Teabag Spirits

Embark on a spooky science adventure with 'Soaring Teabag Spirits'! This exciting experiment showcases the fascinating effect of heat on air movement, using simple tea bags to create ghost-like figures that take flight. Witness the mysterious ascent of these spectral tea bags, and understand the science behind why warm air rises and cool air sinks. Gather your tea bags, markers, and a sense of wonder for this ghostly scientific journey!

Material

- Tea bags
- Baking sheet
- Markers
- Lighter*
- Scissors
- A bowl

Instructions

Step 1 Remove the string holding the tea bags	**Step 2** Open the tea bags and use a bowl to empty their content	**Step 3** Smooth the tea bags and draw ghost face on them using the markers
Step 4 Open up the tea bags and place them on the baking sheet with the opening facing downwards	**Step 5** Light the top of the tea bags with a lighter and step back	**Step 6** When the fire reaches the base of the tea bag, your ghosts will shoot into the air, and the ashes will land back on the baking sheet

*Seek adult help and ensure a fire extinguisher is in place.

Science

● **Igniting the Teabag**: Lighting the top of the tea bag starts the process. The heat from the flame causes the air molecules inside the tea bag to become energetic and move faster.

◉ **Air Movement**: As the air molecules heat up, they start moving quickly, spreading upwards and out of the tea bag.

⬆ **Warm Air Rises**: The heated air inside the tea bag becomes less dense than the cooler air outside. Since warm air is lighter, it rises above the cooler, denser air.

🍃 **Density Difference**: The key to the tea bags' flight is the difference in density between the warm air inside and the cool air outside. The greater the difference, the stronger the lift.

🕊 **Ghostly Flight**: This difference in air density creates a lifting force, causing the tea bags to rise like ghosts, demonstrating a basic principle of thermodynamics.

Explore further

Different Shapes and Sizes: Try the experiment with tea bags of various shapes and sizes. Observe how the shape and size of the tea bag affect how it flies. Do larger tea bags rise higher or slower?

Weight Experiments: Add small, light objects like a paper clip or a piece of thread to the tea bag. See how added weight influences the flight. Does it fly higher, lower, or not at all?

Airflow Observations: Perform the experiment in different areas with varying airflow, like near a window or in a more enclosed space. Notice how air currents in the room impact the tea bags' flight.

Flame Positioning: Experiment with lighting the tea bag from different sides or angles. Does changing the point where the flame starts affect the way the tea bag rises?

(19) Rainbow Water Bridge

Embark on a colorful journey with the 'Rainbow Water Bridge' experiment! Discover how water can magically 'walk' across cups, creating a stunning spectrum of rainbow colors. This fascinating activity demonstrates the power of adhesion and cohesion in water molecules, allowing water to flow along a paper towel pathway from one cup to another. Get ready to blend science and art as you watch a vibrant rainbow water bridge form before your eyes!

Material

+ Paper towel
+ 7 transparent cups
+ Food colouring (red, yellow, blue)
+ Tap water

Instructions

Step 1
Place empty transparent 7 cups next to each other

Step 2
Fill the 1st, 3rd, 5th, and 7th cup with water. About ¾ full

Step 3
Add 6 drops of red food coloring to the 1st and 7th cups

Step 4
Add 6 drops of yellow food coloring in the 3rd cup

Step 5
Add 6 drops of blue food coloring in the 5th cup

Step 6
Take 6 paper towel sheets and double fold them in half lengthwise into 2" strips

Step 7
Dip one end of the first folded paper towel in the first cup, and the other end into the second cup. The ends should touch the bottom of the cups

Step 8
Dip one end the second folded paper towel in the 2nd cup, and the other end in the 3rd cup. Continue with the remaining folded paper towels until the last one is dipped in the 6th cup from one end and the 7th cup from the other end

Step 9
Watch as the colored water starts walking through the paper towels and into the empty cups. The colors will start to mix in the empty cups. Leave the experiment running for 1-hour

Science

Capillary Action: The process that makes water 'walk' is known as capillary action, allowing liquid to flow in narrow spaces without the assistance of external forces.

Cohesion Effect: Cohesion is the scientific term for the tendency of water molecules to stick to each other, thanks to hydrogen bonding.

Adhesion Effect: Adhesion occurs when water molecules also stick to other materials, like the fibers in a paper towel.

Balance of Forces: Capillary action happens when the force of adhesion (water sticking to the paper) is stronger than the force of cohesion (water sticking to itself).

Cellulose Fibers: Paper towels are made from cellulose fibers, which have small spaces acting like tubes to draw water up.

Defying Gravity: Water can travel upward against gravity because it adheres to the walls of these tiny spaces, similar to how water moves from a plant's roots to its leaves.

Explore further

Water Levels: Experiment with varying the water levels in the cups, from half-filled to nearly full. Note how different water amounts affect the speed and flow of the capillary action.

Color Mixing Magic: Pay close attention to how primary colors mix in the empty cups to create secondary colors. Record which colors blend to form new ones and experiment with different primary color placements to achieve a variety of secondary shades.

Paper Towel Types: Try using different brands or types of paper towels. Observe if the thickness or texture changes the rate at which water travels or affects the color blending.

(20) Glowing Homemade Lava Lamp

Unleash a dazzling science display with the 'Glowing Homemade Lava Lamp'! This experiment illuminates the fascinating principle that oil and water don't mix, thanks to their different densities. You can create a mesmerizing, effervescent lava lamp with simple ingredients from around your home. Watch as the vibrant colors dance and glitter sparkles in a groovy glow, all while gaining a visual understanding of density and buoyancy. Shine a light on science as you craft this radiant reaction right in your jar!

Material

- Clear jar with a lid
- Tap water
- Food colouring
- Salt
- Glitter
- Vegetable oil
- Flashlight

Instructions

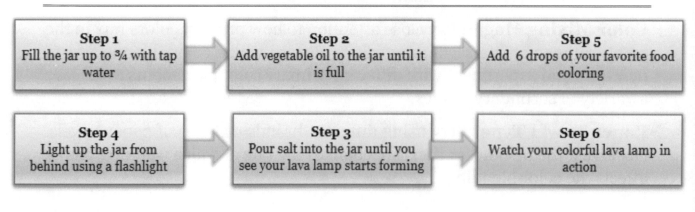

Step 1
Fill the jar up to ¾ with tap water

Step 2
Add vegetable oil to the jar until it is full

Step 5
Add 6 drops of your favorite food coloring

Step 4
Light up the jar from behind using a flashlight

Step 3
Pour salt into the jar until you see your lava lamp starts forming

Step 6
Watch your colorful lava lamp in action

Science

Oil vs. Water: Oil is less dense than water, so it floats on top. This difference in density creates distinct layers in your lava lamp.

Salt's Sinking Effect: Salt is denser than both oil and water. When you sprinkle salt into the lamp, it sinks through the oil and into the water.

Fizzing Action: Adding salt to the water generates carbon dioxide bubbles. This is because the salt initiates a reaction that releases the gas.

Rising Bubbles: The carbon dioxide bubbles cling to the colored water droplets, pulling them up through the oil towards the top of the jar.

Colorful Descent: After the carbon dioxide bubbles burst at the surface, the density of the colored water causes it to sink back down.

Explore further

Salt Quantity Experiment

Try using varying quantities of salt. Record how different amounts influence the rate at which the colored water blobs rise and fall. Does more salt speed up or slow down the reaction?

Sealed Jar Observation

After adding salt, seal the jar with its lid. Watch the bubbles' behavior at the surface. What differences do you observe when the jar is closed versus open?

Temperature Test

Conduct the experiment at different temperatures. Use warm water and then cold water to see how temperature affects the movement of oil, water, and the reaction with salt.

Light Effects

Shine lights of different colors through your lava lamp. Note any changes in how the colors of the lamp appear and how the light affects the visibility of the reaction.

(21) Baked Ice Cream

Delve into the delicious mystery of 'Baked Ice Cream'! It may seem impossible, but you can actually bake ice cream without it turning into a puddle. The secret lies in encasing your ice cream with a protective meringue layer. This fluffy armor acts as an insulator, deflecting the oven's heat and keeping the ice cream chilly and firm. You'll see how this sweet barrier works magic in the oven by whipping up a simple meringue and enveloping a scoop of your favorite ice cream. Ready to beat the heat with this cool culinary experiment?

Material

- 3 egg whites
- ½ cup of sugar
- A cup of ice cream
- A large cookie
- Aluminum foil
- A baking sheet

Instructions*

Step 1 Preheat your oven to 500 °F (260 °C)	**Step 2** Use aluminum foil to cover the baking sheet	**Step 3** Whisk the 3 egg whites until they form stiff peaks
Step 4 Add sugar, 1 tablespoon at a time, and whisk again. Continue to add sugar and whisk until your meringue is thick and glossy	**Step 5** Place a large cookie on the baking sheet and add your ice cream on the top of the cookie	**Step 6** Spread the meringue prepared in Step 4 all over the ice cream. Make sure to leave no exposed spots
Step 7 Use the lower rack of your oven to bake the mixture	**Step 8** Bake for 3-5 minutes until the meringue is a bit brown	**Step 9** Remove your baked ice cream from the oven and enjoy its amazing taste!

*Seek an adult's help when you handle the oven.

Science

⬤ **Meringue Magic**: Meringue, made from whipped egg whites and sugar, forms a protective insulating layer around the ice cream.

◯ **Airy Barrier**: Beating the egg whites incorporates air into the meringue. This air-filled mixture acts as an efficient insulator.

◉ **Heat Transfer**: Normally, heat moves quickly through dense materials. But in airy substances like meringue, heat transfer slows down significantly.

▮ **Gaseous Gap**: Air, being a gas, pushes the meringue's molecules apart, creating more space between them and hindering heat conduction.

▦ **Protecting Ice Cream**: The air pockets trapped in the meringue create a barrier that slows down the heat from the oven, preventing the ice cream from melting.

Explore further

Meringue Thickness Test

Experiment with different thicknesses of the meringue layer. Try a thin layer, then a thicker one. Observe how the thickness affects the ice cream's ability to stay frozen in the oven.

Whipping Techniques

Change how long you whip the egg whites. Compare a less whipped meringue with one that's whipped until very stiff. Does the amount of air in the meringue change how well it insulates?

Oven Temperature Variation

Bake the meringue-covered ice cream at different oven temperatures. Note how varying temperatures impact the insulating effectiveness of the meringue.

Flavor Experiments

Use different flavors of ice cream. See if the flavor or ingredients of the ice cream (like chunks of fruit or chocolate) influence how well the meringue insulates.

Fun Facts: Ice Cream Sience

🥄 **Ideal Serving Temperature**: Ice cream is best enjoyed between -10°C and -15°C, optimizing flavor and texture.

❄️ **Freezing Point Depression**: Sugar in ice cream lowers its freezing point, preventing it from freezing solid and keeping it creamy.

🥄 **Scoopability Factor**: The balance of ingredients and temperature determines how easily ice cream can be scooped.

🎲 🍓 **Flavor Carriers**: Fats in ice cream help carry and enhance various flavors, making them more pronounced.

🌿 **Vanilla Effect**: Vanilla is often added to balance sweetness and add depth to other flavors.

🍫 **Mix-ins**: Ingredients like chocolate chips or nuts add texture contrasts and complex flavors.

🧊 **Ice Crystal Formation**: Small ice crystals give ice cream its smooth texture; rapid freezing helps achieve this.

🧈 **Role of Air**: Air is whipped into ice cream during churning, making it light and fluffy; premium ice creams have less air.

🥛 **Fat Content**: Fat in ice cream (from dairy) contributes to creaminess and flavor richness.

Taste Perception: The cold temperature of ice cream can temporarily numb the taste buds, slightly muting flavors, which is why ice cream often has high levels of sugar and flavorings.

Color Appeal: Visual appeal is key; the colors in ice cream can enhance the perception of its flavor. For instance, pink is often associated with strawberry or cherry flavors.

Texture Variety: The contrast in textures, from creamy bases to crunchy mix-ins, plays a significant role in the overall sensory enjoyment of ice cream.

Nutritional Content: Ice cream can be a source of calcium and protein but is also high in sugar and fat. Balance and moderation are key in consumption.

Dietary Variations: There are now various ice cream alternatives available for different dietary needs, including dairy-free, sugar-free, and vegan options.

Incorporating Fruits: Adding fruits to ice cream not only enhances flavor but also boosts its nutritional value with vitamins, minerals, and fibers.

Shelf Life: While ice cream can be stored for long periods, over time it can develop ice crystals or lose its texture and flavor due to temperature fluctuations.

Preventing Freezer Burn: Freezer burn, which affects texture and taste, can be minimized by storing ice cream in airtight containers and avoiding repeated thawing and refreezing.

(22) Cloud in a Bottle

Unlock the secrets of the sky with 'Coud in a Bottle'! Have you ever wondered how those fluffy clouds in the sky form? It all starts with condensation, the same process that makes water droplets appear on a cold drink on a warm day. In this fascinating experiment, you'll recreate the natural process that forms clouds using simple household items. Watch as warm water, a cool surface, and a little smoke come together to form a mini cloud right in your jar. Get ready to capture a piece of the sky in your hands!

Material

+ A glass jar
+ Warm water
+ Plastic ice pack
+ A spoon
+ Matches

Instructions*

Step 1	Step 2	Step 3
Pour warm water into the glass jar (around 2" (5 cm) of water)	Light a match and blow it out so it smokes, and drop it into the jar	Place an ice pack on the top of the jar to close it and watch your cloud starts forming near the top of the jar

*Seek adult help when you use matches.

Science

💧 **Water Molecules**: Cloud formation begins with water molecules, which are essential for creating the droplets that make up a cloud.

⚪ **Cloud Condensation Nuclei**: These are small particles like dust or atmospheric pollution. Water vapor condenses around these nuclei to form clouds.

🌡️ **Temperature/Pressure Changes**: Clouds often form when warm air rises, cools down, and encounters lower atmospheric pressure.

🚀 **Rising Warm Air**: In the atmosphere, as warm air rises and cools, the water vapor starts to condense around the cloud condensation nuclei.

💧 **Smoke as Nuclei**: In this experiment, smoke particles from a blown-out match act as cloud condensation nuclei, enabling water vapor in the warm air inside the jar to condense and form a visible cloud.

🌥️ **Visible Cloud Formation**: The condensed water droplets around the smoke particles create a miniature cloud inside the bottle, demonstrating how clouds form in nature.

Explore further

Temperature Effects: Experiment with various temperatures of warm water, ensuring it's below the boiling point. Observe how different water temperatures impact the cloud's formation and density.

Removing the Ice Pack: Try taking the ice pack off the jar and watch the cloud's behavior. Can you explain why the cloud dissipates when the cooling source is removed?

Smoke Variation: Use different sources for cloud condensation nuclei, like incense smoke or a different type of match. Note if different smoke sources affect the cloud formation.

Jar Size Experiment: Conduct the experiment in jars of different sizes. Does a larger or smaller jar change how the cloud forms or how long it lasts?

(23) Eggshell Stepping Challenge

Discover the surprising strength of everyday eggs in the 'Eggshell Stepping Challenge'! It might seem impossible, but with the right technique, you can actually walk on eggs without cracking them. This experiment puts the remarkable architectural design of eggshells to the test, showing how their unique shape allows for an even distribution of pressure. Be ready for potential spills in this egg-citing adventure – grab some protective sheets, enlist an assistant, and step into the world of practical physics with a dozen eggs under your feet!"

Material

- 2 dozen large eggs in two cartoons
- Sheets or old clothing
- A knife
- An assistant

Instructions*

Step 1 Check the eggs carefully for cracks. Replace any cracked egg	**Step 2** Remove the center bits of the egg carton to make them leveled with the top of the eggs	**Step 3** Make sure that the all the eggs have the same direction, either the pointy end or the rounded end facing up
Step 4 Spread a sheet on the floor and place the egg cartoons on it side by side. Each side for one foot	**Step 5** Place one bare foot onto the first cartoon. Make sure to place your foot flat, such that your body weight is distributed evenly across the eggs	**Step 6** Ask your assistant to hold your hand and place your other bare foot on the second cartoon. Ask your assistant to capture a photo of your standing on eggs!

*Seek an adult's help when you use the knife.

Science

🥚 **Egg Architecture**: Eggs have a unique structure, with internal forces pushing inward evenly across the shell, contributing to their strength.

🌐 **Curved Design**: The curved shape of the egg distributes pressure evenly. This design makes the shell strong under certain conditions.

💔 **Vulnerability to Uneven Forces**: While eggs are strong under even pressure, they crack easily under uneven forces, like when struck against a hard surface.

🏛 **Arch Support**: The rounded ends of the egg form an arch-like structure, similar to architectural arches, providing support and strength.

⚖ **Weight Distribution**: When standing on eggs, their shape helps spread your weight evenly, allowing them to support more weight without breaking.

Explore further

Crack Analysis: If any eggs cracked during the experiment, examine them. What could explain why these particular eggs broke? Consider factors like the egg's position, the way the weight was applied, or differences in the shell's structure.

Egg Arrangement: Rearrange the eggs in different patterns or formations. Test if certain arrangements offer more stability or are more prone to cracking under weight.

Egg Size and Type: Experiment with eggs of different sizes or types (such as chicken, duck, or quail eggs). Do larger or smaller eggs show differences in strength?

Surface Experiment: Conduct the experiment on different surfaces, like a soft carpet or a hard floor. Note how the surface beneath the eggs affects their ability to withstand weight.

(24) Smartphone Sound Amplifier

Discover the power of acoustics with the 'Smartphone Sound Amplifier'! You don't need expensive technology to boost your smartphone's sound. In this creative experiment, you'll see how simple household items can be transformed into an effective sound amplifier. By using a cardboard tube and a pair of plastic cups, you can enhance your smartphone's audio output. Get ready to amplify your favorite tunes with this innovative and fun DIY project!

Material

+ Cardboard tube
+ 2 plastic cups
+ A smartphone
+ Scissors

Instructions

Step 1 Cut holes on the side of the plastic cups to fit the cardboard tube in.	**Step 2** Hold the cardboard tube and attach a cup to each end of the tube	**Step 3** Cut a thin slit on the top of the cardboard tube just enough to hold the smartphone
Step 4 Check where the smartphone speaker is located (top or bottom)	**Step 5** Insert the smartphone in the slot. Make sure that the side of the smartphone with speaker is in the slot	**Step 6** Play music on the smartphone and enjoy the amplified sound!

Science

Sound Wave Journey: Sound travels in waves that can be manipulated to enhance audio quality, project voices, create effects, or amplify volume.

Amplification: An amplifier takes these sound waves and increases their amplitude to make sounds richer, deeper, and louder.

Natural Dispersion: By default, sound waves radiate outward in all directions from the source of the sound.

Directional Control: Similar to how cupping your hands around your mouth focuses sound forward, we can direct sound waves.

Smartphone Acoustics: When a smartphone plays music, the sound spreads out. Placing it in a cardboard tube channels these waves towards the plastic cups.

Cup Speakers: The plastic cups act like speakers, focusing the sound waves in one direction, naturally amplifying the sound as it exits the setup.

Explore further

Tube Length Test: Use cardboard tubes of various lengths and observe how they affect the sound. Does a longer or shorter tube change the quality or volume of the amplified sound?

Cup Materials: Try replacing the plastic cups with cups made of different materials, such as paper or foam. Note any differences in sound amplification and quality.

Tube Diameter: Experiment with tubes of different diameters to see if the width of the tube influences the sound. Is there a difference in sound amplification between wider and narrower tubes?

Cup Size and Shape: Use cups of different sizes and shapes. How does the cup's size and shape affect the sound's direction and quality?

(25) Crisp Keeper: Homemade Fresh Cookies

Unlock the secret to everlasting crunch with the 'Lasting Crispy Cookies'! Isn't it disappointing when delicious homemade cookies go from crispy to soft? The culprit is often moisture from the air. Like commercial cookies sealed for freshness, you too can maintain that delightful crisp using a little science trick. In this experiment, you'll bake a batch of cookies and then employ a clever method to keep them crispy for days. So, preheat your ovens and get ready to combine the art of baking with the science of preservation!

Material

- 2 cup flour
- 1 teaspoon baking powder
- ½ teaspoon salt
- 1 stick of unsalted butter
- ½ cup sugar
- Baking sheets

- 1 egg
- 2 tablespoon water
- ½ teaspoon lemon juice
- 1 loaf of fresh bread
- Electric mixer
- Baking pan

Instructions*

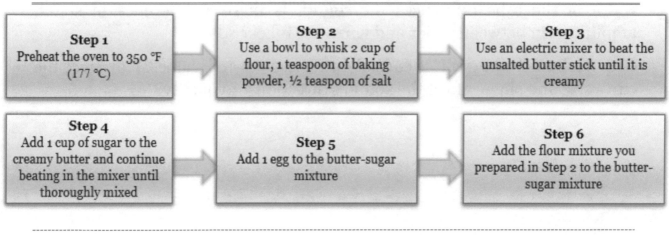

Step 1
Preheat the oven to 350 °F (177 °C)

Step 2
Use a bowl to whisk 2 cup of flour, 1 teaspoon of baking powder, ½ teaspoon of salt

Step 3
Use an electric mixer to beat the unsalted butter stick until it is creamy

Step 4
Add 1 cup of sugar to the creamy butter and continue beating in the mixer until thoroughly mixed

Step 5
Add 1 egg to the butter-sugar mixture

Step 6
Add the flour mixture you prepared in Step 2 to the butter-sugar mixture

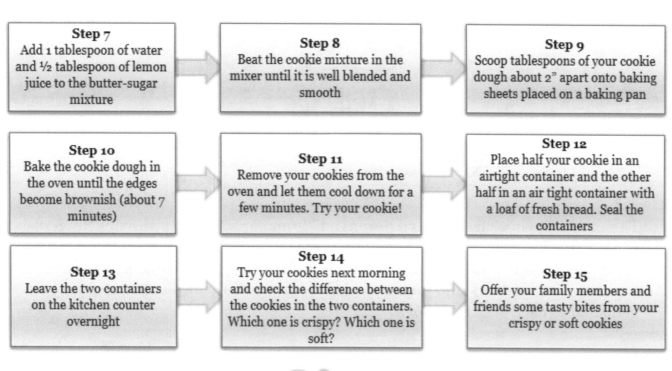

Step 7
Add 1 tablespoon of water and ½ tablespoon of lemon juice to the butter-sugar mixture

Step 8
Beat the cookie mixture in the mixer until it is well blended and smooth

Step 9
Scoop tablespoons of your cookie dough about 2" apart onto baking sheets placed on a baking pan

Step 10
Bake the cookie dough in the oven until the edges become brownish (about 7 minutes)

Step 11
Remove your cookies from the oven and let them cool down for a few minutes. Try your cookie!

Step 12
Place half your cookie in an airtight container and the other half in an air tight container with a loaf of fresh bread. Seal the containers

Step 13
Leave the two containers on the kitchen counter overnight

Step 14
Try your cookies next morning and check the difference between the cookies in the two containers. Which one is crispy? Which one is soft?

Step 15
Offer your family members and friends some tasty bites from your crispy or soft cookies

Science

🧊 **Bread Hardens**: Leaving bread out allows its moisture to evaporate into the air, making it hard due to its less dense texture and lower sugar content.

🍪 **Cookies Soften**: Cookies, rich in sugar, draw moisture from the air because of their hygroscopic nature, softening as they absorb water vapor.

🍬 **Sugar's Role**: The high sugar concentration in cookies makes them hygroscopic, meaning they naturally absorb moisture from their environment.

💧 **Moisture Dynamics**: A cookie's dense structure holds onto the moisture it absorbs, changing its texture from crisp to soft.

🥄➕🍪 **Bread and Cookies Together**: When bread and cookies share an airtight container, the bread's evaporating moisture is absorbed by the cookies, keeping them soft.

✋ **Isolating Cookies**: Cookies in an airtight container without bread stay crispy longer because there's limited moisture for them to absorb.

Future
SmartMinds

Awesome Science Experiments
for Kids

www.futuresmartminds.com

Thank you for choosing "**Future Scientist**" from our **STEM Explorers Series: Ignite the Future**. We sincerely hope that you and your young explorers have embarked on a fruitful learning experience, discovering the wonders of science together. Your journey into inquiry and discovery is truly invaluable, and we are delighted to have been a part of it.

If you found this adventure enriching, we would be deeply appreciative **if you could take a moment to rate "Future Scientist" on Amazon.** Your feedback is not only a tremendous support to us, but it also guides other curious minds to explore the fascinating world of STEM.

Scan to Rate Us on Amazon

We invite you and your aspiring learner to continue this enriching journey with the other titles in our series. Each book is crafted to open up new horizons of knowledge and imagination:

⚙ "**Future Engineer**" for a hands-on exploration into the world of engineering,

🔢 "**Future Mathematician**" to unlock the intriguing puzzles of mathematics,

🔍 "**Future Chef**" to blend the art of cooking with scientific discovery,

🤖 "**Future AI Expert**" to step into the realm of artificial intelligence.

Every book is an opportunity to ignite a lifelong passion for learning and discovery. We can't wait to see where your next adventure takes you!

With warm regards,

Future SmartMinds

www.futuresmartminds.com

Please check our other kids' **STEM** activities books!

Available on Amazon!

(Scan the QR code to visit Amazon store)

Introduce your child to the captivating world of engineering." This exceptional book is tailored for budding young minds, ages 7 to 12, and is brimming with astonishing STEM engineering experiments that ignite creativity and critical thinking.

Unleash Engineering Wonders: Engineering is all around us, but sometimes it can seem complex. "**Future Engineer**" bridges this gap by unveiling mind-blowing engineering experiments that use everyday household items, making engineering accessible, exciting, and hands-on. These experiments spark curiosity and develop analytical skills.

Available on Amazon!

(Scan the QR code to visit Amazon store)

Prepare your child for an exciting mathematical journey with "**Future Mathematician**." This extraordinary book is specially crafted for young minds, ages 7 to 12, making mathematics not just accessible but enjoyable, empowering them with the skills they need to tackle real-world math challenges.

Unlocking Mathematical Magic: Mathematics is everywhere around us, but sometimes it can seem disconnected from our daily lives. "**Future Mathematician**" breaks down these barriers, revealing the enchanting world of math that surrounds us every day. This book bridges the gap between the classroom and reality, showing kids the profound importance of math in their lives.

Please check our other kids' **STEM** activities books!

Available on Amazon!

(Scan the QR code to visit Amazon store)

Unleash Your Child's Potential with Artificial Intelligence (AI)! **"Future AI Expert**," where the wonders of artificial intelligence unfold through 20 captivating activities. Designed for young minds aged 7-12, this book offers a thrilling introduction to AI, blending education with a whole lot of interactive fun.

20 Amazing AI Activities: Engage with a variety of projects, from AI-powered storytelling to problem-solving games, each designed to spark curiosity and encourage exploration.

Easy to Follow, Fun to Learn: With kid-friendly instructions, the complex world of AI becomes an exciting playground for young minds.

Available on Amazon!

(Scan the QR code to visit Amazon store)

Prepare to embark on an exciting journey where the joy of **cooking** meets the wonder of **science**! This vibrant cookbook is packed with **25 delicious cooking experiments** crafted for young chefs, aged 7 to 12, offering diverse hands-on experiments across five captivating sections: Bake, Grill, Boil, Fry, and Desserts.

Interactive Learning Experience: With step-by-step instructions, ingredient lists, and required equipment for each cooking experiment, **'Future Chef'** transforms the kitchen into a vivid laboratory. Through vibrant illustrations, scientific principles come alive, ensuring that each recipe is an engaging exploration of culinary science.

Made in United States
Cleveland, OH
29 December 2024

12820064R00042